City Adv

My name is Micky Dare,
and I'm a city boy.

I don't live in the centre of
the city. That's full of big shops,
blocks of offices, cinemas, shows
and advertisements with flashing lights.

I don't live in the suburbs,
either, on one of the big new
housing estates with parks
and grass you can't play on.

No, I'm lucky. I live in
the most exciting part of the city:
down towards the river and docks,
where something is always happening.

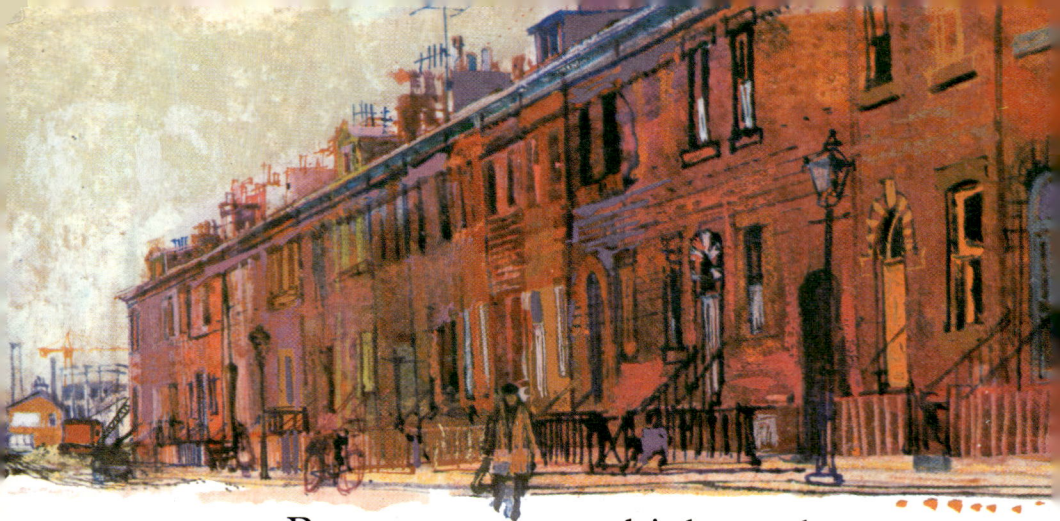

By now you may think you know
which city I'm talking about,
but I'm not telling you.
This adventure story will explain
why I, have to keep quiet
about that. It will also explain
why I don't mind moths!

The house that I live in
is called Two Eight Seven.
It looks just like the others
in the row, with dirty walls
and windows. That's because
of the smoke from the docks
and the gas works, and the fumes
from the factories across the river.

It has rusty railings in front
of the basement, and a little yard
backing on to the next row of houses.

Although we are Two Eight Seven,
the numbers in our street start at
One Nine Five, where my friend
Alf Taylor lives. All the other houses
(and the one behind One Nine Five)
have been pulled down to make way
for new buildings. In a year
or so the rest of the street
will probably be pulled down too.
That's why we don't bother much
about rust, dirt and peeling paint.

Our street is a dead end now.
It doesn't lead anywhere, except
up to the Dump—that's what we call
the clearing where the rest of
the houses used to be. The Dump
would be a good place to play,
but that's not allowed,
because sometimes cranes
and bulldozers and things
are parked there.

All sorts of people live down
our way, but most of them work
in the docks, like my dad.
He used to be a plumber, but he says
he gets more money as a crane driver,
even if he does have to work late
some evenings.

Our next door neighbour on one
side used to be a scrap merchant
named Mr. Vince. Everyone called
him Old Jimmy; not because
his name was Jimmy, but because
he always wore a pair of dirty old
gym shoes. No one liked him much;
he was too mean and crafty.
Although he got most of his junk
for nothing, he always wanted
a lot of money for anything he sold.

Old Jimmy seemed to do pretty well
out of his scrap business.
When he first came to live by us,
he just had a wooden handcart
that he pulled along himself.
After that, he bought a battered old van
which was always going wrong.
Then one day he turned up driving quite
a big truck which looked almost new.

I was sitting on the steps
at the time, making a battleship
from a plastic kit I'd been given
on my last birthday.

Old Jimmy backed his truck up
in front of our house,
and came shuffling across to me.

"Like my new truck, boy?"
he wheezed.

"Not bad," I answered,
thinking he could do with
some new trousers as well.

"Is your dad in?"

I stuck the last gun turret
carefully on the battleship,
and then I answered,

"I think so. Why?"

Old Jimmy winked slyly.
"Go and tell him I want to see him."

I shrugged my shoulders,
then ran up the steps and through
to the kitchen. My dad was having
a cup of tea there.

"Old Jimmy is outside and wants to see you," I said. Then I added, "He's got a blinking great new truck."

"Has he now," said my dad, putting on his boots. "It beats me how he can make that kind of money just collecting junk."

He followed me outside again.

"Morning, Mr. Dare," wheezed Old Jimmy. Then he sniffed loudly and said, "Want a bath?"

My dad walked slowly down
the steps, clenching his fists.

"What did you say?" he growled.

Old Jimmy half grinned and
shuffled off to his truck.
He pulled out a couple of pegs
and the tailboard dropped down.
Lying on a pile of old sacks
was a small white bath.

"Oh!" said my dad, looking
a bit confused. "I see what you mean."

Old Jimmy was rubbing
his dirty hands and grinning away.

"Just what you need," he wheezed.
"And no trouble to fit when you've
been a plumber."

"No thanks," my dad said, curtly.
"We've done without a bathroom here
for the past five years, and we can
do without for a bit longer,
until this place comes down.
It would be a sheer waste of money."

Looking pained, Old Jimmy said,
"I'm not trying to sell this bath.
You can have it for free.
Someone asked me to get rid of it
for them this morning,
and I knew you were a plumber once,
so I thought you might like it."
My dad looked at him suspiciously.
"Come on," he said. "How much?"
"Free. You can have it for nothing."
The words seemed to be choking
Old Jimmy. "Twenty pence then,"
he wheezed, "just to cover the petrol."

"I reckon it would just fit
into the kitchen," commented my dad,
measuring the bath with his eye.
"But twenty pence when it
could be worth a fiver?
What's the catch?"

Old Jimmy spread his hands
and said, "You're my next door
neighbour, and I'm just trying
to do you a good turn."
He sniffed. "There's no catch."

My dad dug into his pockets
and produced some money.

"Right. Ta very much." he said,
stuffing the coins into Old Jimmy's
dirty paw. "Can you give us a hand
with it? Micky, you steady the end
as we slide it out."

It didn't take the three of us long
to get the bath into the kitchen,
although it was heavy enough.

"There," wheezed Old Jimmy,
shoving the side against the wall
where our broken washing machine
had been standing. "Fits a treat.
Worth a tenner of anyone's money,
but I like to do people a good turn
when I can."

He eyed my dad thoughtfully.
"You never know," he continued,
"you might be able to do me
a good turn one day, seeing that
you work in the docks."
Then he winked knowingly, and added,
"Or one night, for that matter."
"Shouldn't have thought so,"
my dad answered uncomfortably.

"Well you never know, do you?"
Old Jimmy was shuffling from one
foot to the other. "Tell you what;
I'll drop round tomorrow with some
extra cheap tobacco I've got hold of.
Then we can have a little chat."

He shuffled out, and my mother
shut the door behind him.

"I don't know that I trust that
dirty old man," she commented.
"Anyway, what do we want with a bath?
There's no proper bathroom here."

"It was too good to turn down
at that price," answered my dad,
kneeling down and examining the fittings.

"It can stand where it is,
and I'll run a waste pipe through
the wall to the outside drain."

"How will we fill it?" I asked.

"We can run a bit of hose from
the sink for the moment,"
my dad told me, standing up.
"Go and get my plumber's tools
from the attic, Micky.
There's a length of old piping
by the water tank; bring that too."

He looked at his watch.
"I'll have the whole thing fixed up
before I go on the evening shift."

When I came down with the tools and piping my mother was fixing up a length of curtain wire. "With plastic curtains across this side, we'll have quite a nice little bathroom," she was saying. "Perhaps Old Jimmy isn't as bad as we think he is after all."

I didn't say anything, but I wasn't so sure about that. Old Jimmy didn't give things away for nothing, I thought to myself, as I watched my dad start boring a hole through the wall. Just what was he going to want in return?

In a couple of hours the waste pipe was attached, and my dad went looking for a bit of hose. Then he remembered the broken washing machine out in the back yard. It had a bit of rubber pipe on it that was exactly the right length.

"There," said my dad, grinning
as he sloshed the bath out
and water gurgled down the plug hole.
"Not bad for twenty pence, is it?
And it'll clean up like new."

He looked at his watch again and
frowned. "Time I was off," he said.
"See you tomorrow morning."
He picked up a packet of sandwiches
from the table, fetched his bike
from the yard, and pushed it through
the passage to the front door.

"Wait a minute," said my mum.
She put her coat on. "I'll walk
as far as the shops with you.
I want to get some plastic sheeting
for those curtains."

Once they had gone, I put the plug
in the bath and turned the sink
cold tap full on. I wasn't too keen
about the idea of having this bath
around the house, but at least
it would make a good test tank
for my warship.

When the water covered the end
of the pipe, I fetched my model
and launched it.

Slowly it turned on its side.

What it really needs is a weight
underneath, I thought, taking it out.

I tried using a bit of putty
my dad had left by the bath,
but it kept sticking to my fingers.

Then I remembered that Alf Taylor
had some plasticine.
That's what I want, I said to myself,
as I wiped the putty off my fingers
with the teatowel.

I went out of the house,
shut the door behind me, and ran down
to One Nine Five. Alf was sitting
on the steps, reading a comic.

"Hi, Alf," I said.
"Got a bit of plasticine to spare?"

"I'll have a look," he answered.
"What do you want it for?"

We went up to his room
and I explained about the new bath,
and trying to make my battleship float.

Alf poked about in his
chest of drawers, and after a while
he produced a little strip of plasticine.

"Thanks; that's fine," I said,
holding out my hand.

Alf closed his fist tightly.
"What's it worth to you?"
he demanded.

I blinked. "Come off it," I said.
"You're getting more like Old Jimmy
every day."

Alf pulled up his coat collar,
hunched his shoulders and shuffled
about. "Well, sir; very difficult
to come by, sir, this plasticine,"
he wheezed. "I really couldn't
let you have it for less than—
less than one of those wine gums
you've got hidden in your pocket."

"You don't miss much," I laughed,
pulling out the packet.

"Ta," said Alf, taking three.
"They stuck to each other,"
he explained calmly. "Here's your
plasticine. And what about coming
to the Docks cinema tonight?
There's a super cowboy film on."

I shook my head. "No money,"
I admitted.

Alf shifted his wine gums from
one cheek to the other, and then
produced a one pound note.
"Just been paid for my paper round,"
he said. "I'll treat you, mate."

"Wow! That's great," I answered.
"But I'll have to see if my mum
wants anything done tonight first.
She'll be home again by now."

Suddenly I choked.

"Swallowed your wine gum?"
Alf asked, seriously.

"The bath," I spluttered.
"I'm not sure that I didn't
leave the tap running!"

"Oh, you wouldn't do a thing
like that," began Alf, grinning,
but I was half-way down the stairs;
I had a nasty feeling
that I was in trouble.

"See you about seven," Alf yelled,
as I shot out into the street.

Our front door was wide open when
I raced up the steps of Two Eight
Seven, and that was a bad sign.
I crept along the passage and gulped.
    There was my mum
on her hands and knees, mopping up.
Water was everywhere.
It was trickling down the steps
leading to the cellar, and soaking
into the carpet in the front room.

My mum stood up to squeeze out
the cloth and saw me standing there.

"Bed, Micky," she said.

"But mum, Alf Taylor says he'll
treat me to the pictures tonight . . ."

"Bed."

"I'm sorry about the mess."

"You'll be sorrier when your dad
hears about it tomorrow.
And just look at my tea towel. *Bed!*"

31

It's no use arguing, I thought,
and climbed slowly up the stairs
to my room. I felt mad at being sent
to bed when Alf was going to treat me
to that cowboy film. He would be
hanging about waiting for me, too.

I took off my jacket, but then
I put it back on again.
Slowly a plan was forming in my mind.
It just wasn't fair being sent to bed
at my age, and I was going
to do something about it.

If only I could get out of the house,
I might still be able to see that film.
My dad wouldn't be back till late,
and mum would be watching the telly.
She wouldn't be up to say goodnight
because I was in disgrace.

I opened the bedroom door and
listened. Mum was still mopping up
in the kitchen, and I couldn't risk
being seen creeping downstairs.

Shutting the door quietly,
I tiptoed along to the box room.
I looked up at the skylight.
Once my dad had been through it
on to the roof to fix the gutter,
and had talked about a ledge there,
running the length of the street.

It was worth taking a look at,
I thought, as I climbed up
on to the water tank. Especially
as one of the three fire escapes in
the row was behind Alf's house!

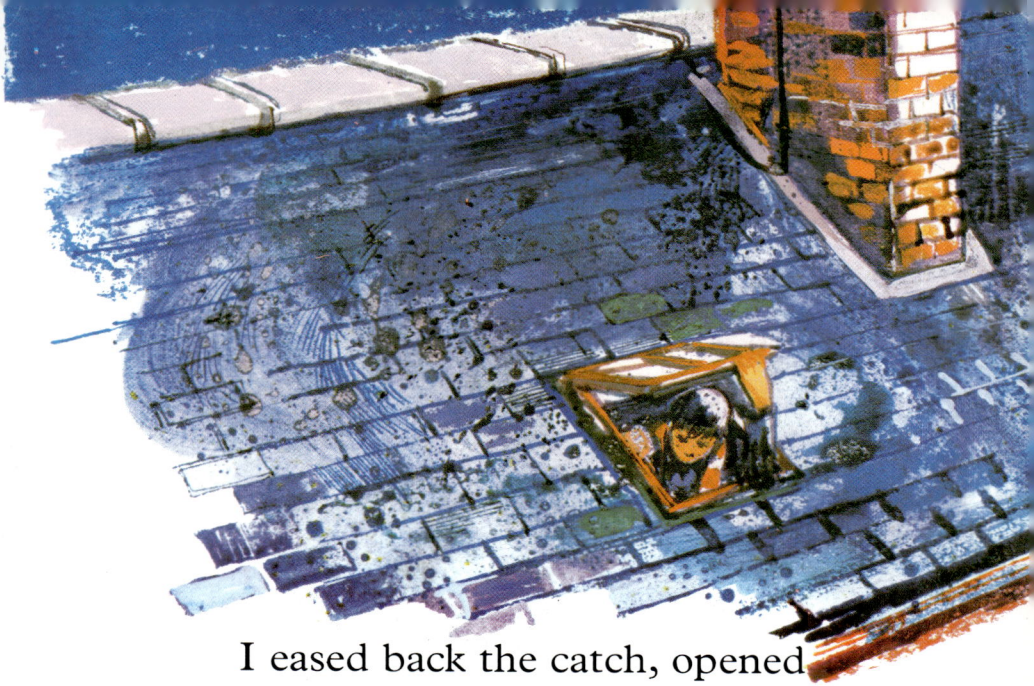

I eased back the catch, opened
the skylight and poked my head out.
Suddenly there was a loud splashing
noise underneath me, and I nearly
fell down with fright. It was only
the water tank filling up, though.

I paused. There was the ledge,
along the top. It couldn't be seen
from the street, but if I fell,
or even if I got caught
climbing about on the roof
when I was supposed to be in bed,
I'd be in trouble. Real trouble!

Then I thought of Alf's face
when he saw me. I grinned to myself,
and climbed right out on to the roof.
There was a woman in one back yard
getting in her washing,
but, luckily, she didn't look up.
I ducked behind a chimney,
waited until she had gone in,
and then crawled along the ledge.

Five minutes later I reached
the end of the row. I could see
a crane and a lorry below in the Dump,
and it looked a horribly long way down.

Crawling to the gutter, I saw
iron railings below: the fire escape.
It wasn't difficult to find
the top rail with my feet,
and then drop safely to the platform.

It was right outside a window,
and as I landed with a loud clang!
my heart missed a beat. A startled face
was staring straight at me.
Then it broke into a grin.

It was Alf.

He slid the window up
and I climbed into his room.

"Where's the fire, Mick?" he asked.
"Keep your voice down," I whispered.
"I'm not supposed to be here."

Alf's jaw fell open as I told him
what had happened.

"But we can still go to that film,"
I ended. "I'll get back the same way
that I got out."

There was an uncomfortable silence,
and then Alf said, "I—I can't
come out tonight after all."

"Why not?"

"Well, I may have to baby-sit,"
replied Alf, uneasily. "And anyway,
you'd never get up the street
without being seen."

I flushed. "Scared, are you?"
I challenged. "I'd get up the street
all right. I've a good mind
to go as far as the Docks cinema
just to show you."

"You wouldn't dare, Dare."

It was a bad joke,
but I was in no mood to back down.

"Right," I said grimly, and swung
one leg over the window sill again.

Alf went pale. "Don't be a fool, Mick," he urged. "You're asking for trouble. You might even run into your dad down that way. Get back home while you can."

He held up his hand and listened. "Quick," he whispered. "I think my mum's coming up the stairs."

I was back on the fire escape and creeping down the iron rungs before the words were out of his mouth. Alf's mum was the last person I wanted to meet just then!

As I reached the ground,
I heard Alf's window slam shut.
Looking up, I saw him draw the curtains.
I was on my own now.

What a fool I had been to say
that I could get to the Docks cinema
and back, I thought. Now I had to do it,
or be laughed at in the morning.

The sun was setting,
and shadows were growing
around Alf's back yard.
There was still about
an hour of daylight left,
I decided, so perhaps
I could get to the cinema
and back before dark.
I didn't fancy climbing
about on the roof at night.

But how was I going to
get into the street?
I couldn't go through
Alf's house.

The only other way was
over the back wall into the Dump.

Everything was quiet. I took
a deep breath, raced for the wall,
and jumped.

My fingers clung to the top,
one foot found a brick sticking out,
and I was up and over, crouching
in the shadow of a parked truck.

It looked familiar, and then
my mouth went dry. It was Old Jimmy's
new truck, and straight ahead of me,
talking to a workman in a cloth cap,
stood Old Jimmy himself.

It just wasn't my day, I thought.

The two men turned and walked
slowly towards me, talking in low voices.
I looked round desperately for
somewhere to hide, but I was cornered.

Then I noticed that the tailboard
of the truck was down, and the pile
of old sacks was still lying there.
As the men drew level with the bonnet,
I climbed into the back and hurriedly
pulled some sacks on top of me.

"See you later, then," I heard
Old Jimmy mutter.

The tailboard banged shut and
the engine started up. To my horror
I felt the truck begin to move,
but then I remembered that the only
way out of the Dump was up our street.
Nobody was going to spot me now!

Once we were well clear
of the street I stuck my head out
and was just in time to see
the Docks cinema going past.

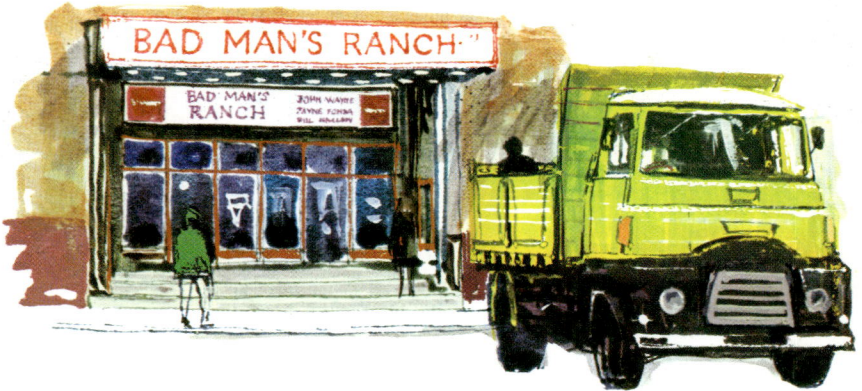

All I needed now was a lift back,
and I had won my dare, I thought.

Now we were turning left, and
a few minutes later I pulled the sacks
over me again as we passed slowly
through the entrance to the docks.

The truck drew up in the shadow of
some crates, and Old Jimmy got out.

I hope he doesn't hang about here
too long, I thought, moving the sacks
aside to see what he was doing.

Old Jimmy was fiddling about
with one of those winking lamps
that are used to warn people
you have a puncture or a breakdown.

What's that for, I wondered.
We haven't broken down.

Again I pulled the sacks over
myself as Old Jimmy shuffled round
to the back of the lorry.

Clunk! He dropped something over
the tailboard, and got back in the cab.

We were moving again.
I lifted the sacks and to my surprise
saw the lamp still winking away
in the far corner. For a moment
I wondered if it was some kind
of signal, but then I realised
that no one could see inside the truck.
Old Jimmy must have forgotten
to turn the lamp off, I thought.

We crawled past a crane
and along the side of the dock.

A few **ya**rds out a foreign cargo boat
was nosing her way towards her berth.
I could just see a foreign seaman
standing on the end of the bridge,
waiting for orders.

Now the ship was almost touching
the dock walls and there was a
ringing of bells and clanking of chains
as she stopped moving.

The man on the bridge raised
his hand in some sort of signal;
we turned slowly away, and thud!
something landed in the truck
and rolled towards me.

Immediately Old Jimmy revved up
and drove off.

Once we were out of the docks
I crawled clear of the sacks.
It was fairly dark by now,
and so long as I kept down
I couldn't very well be seen.

Feeling around, I touched
the object that had landed
in the truck, and picked up
a heavy brown paper parcel.
One corner seemed to have been
torn open as it fell.

I held the parcel up and gasped.
In the light of passing street lamps
I saw lots of small white packets inside.

My mind raced. That lamp;
it could only be seen from the bridge
of the ship. It *had* been a signal!
But what were these little packets?

Could Old Jimmy be mixed up
in a dope or drug racket?

I've been reading too many comics,
I decided, as the truck drove up
our street again. I kept well down
until we turned into the Dump.
Then as we came to a stop,
I scrambled over the side of the truck
and looked round for the back wall
of Alf's house.

There it was—and there was
Cloth Cap, not five yards away,
walking towards me!

I doubled up and ran across
the Dump, making for a crane.
Perhaps I could hide underneath
until the coast was clear.

"Got the stuff?" Cloth Cap hissed.

"It's in the back,"
I heard Old Jimmy mutter.
The tailboard creaked as they let it down.

"The light's still on,"
protested Cloth Cap.

Old Jimmy chuckled. "So what?"
he said softly. "No one can see it
except from above. Worked like magic."

There was a rustle of notes
as Cloth Cap handed over some money.
So that was why Old Jimmy
was doing so well these days.
He was mixed up in smuggling!

"Now," said Cloth Cap.
"We'll just load that crate of scrap
on to your truck, and then
we've got an alibi in case
of any awkward questions."

"Yeah," said Old Jimmy, cackling.
"That's the load I picked up
from the docks!" He paused.
"But how do I get it on my truck?"
   "Easy," Cloth Cap replied.
"It's right by the crane.
I'll drop it on for you."
   I glanced round. Right beside
the crane where I was hiding
stood a large wooden crate.
It was about time I got clear.
   "Back your truck up,"
I heard Cloth Cap say
as he started to cross the Dump.

I hesitated. If these men
were smugglers, then I ought
to go for the police,
but if I was making a mistake,
I was sure to get a good hiding
for what I'd been up to!

Cloth Cap reached the crane,
climbed up the steps,
and got in the cab. I had hesitated
too long: I would have to wait
until they had gone, now.

The truck backed up to the crane
and Old Jimmy climbed out.

"What about the noise?"
he called anxiously.

"Don't worry about that,"
muttered Cloth Cap.
"Just get the hook under the ropes."
The crane's motor came to life,
and the hook dropped down
on top of the crate.
It sounded like a lorry engine;
and no one in our street would bother
about a noise like that.
Why doesn't a policeman or someone
come along, I thought miserably.
"Hurry up," hissed Cloth Cap.
"I can't get this hook on;
give me a hand," wheezed Old Jimmy,
struggling away on top of the crate.
Cloth Cap muttered something,
got down, and joined Old Jimmy
on top of the scrap.

Hope my dad's not home yet,
I thought to myself,
and then suddenly I remembered
what Old Jimmy had said about favours,
and coming to our house tomorrow.

Just suppose my dad found himself
helping smugglers without knowing it.

He might end up in prison!

I had to make sure that
these two were caught. But how?

Without really thinking
what I was going to do next,
I slipped out from under the crane,
climbed up the side, and eased
myself into the control cab.

There was a dull, reflected light
from the city in the sky,
and I could see all the levers
and dials. But what now?

"Hey!" whispered Cloth Cap,
glancing up. "Someone's in the crane.
Get him, quick!"

If only I knew
which lever to pull, I thought,
looking round desperately.

Something soft dropped on my hand.
Sitting there, waving his feelers,
was the biggest moth I have ever seen.

For a moment I thought it was
a giant spider! I jumped a mile
and flung out my arms
to get rid of the thing,
crashing against the controls.

Suddenly there was a grinding roar.
The cab rocked as the motor raced,
and the crate rocketed into the air.

"Help! Stop it!" the two men
yelled, but I couldn't do a thing;
I didn't know which lever I had hit.

Now the two were twenty feet up,
and shouting with fear. Crunch!
The chain jammed in the top wheel
of the crane, the motor stalled,
and the crate stayed there,
swinging gently to and fro.

"Get us down,"
I heard Old Jimmy wheezing. "Help!"
But I was already back on the ground,
and running for the wall.

One or two lights started to come on
and curtains were being drawn aside
as I raced up the fire escape again.

The glow in the sky
from the city lights showed me
the way back on to the roof.
It also outlined the swinging crate
and the two frightened figures
clinging to it, yelling away.

Somewhere a window shot up,
and a voice shouted,
"Hang on, mate; you'll be all right.
We're getting the cops!"

I was still grinning about this
as I dropped through the skylight
back on to the water tank in our attic.
Then my smile faded. I still had
worries of my own. Supposing
my mum had been up to see me!

I crept back into my bedroom,
threw my clothes on the floor,
quickly pulled on my pyjamas,
and jumped into bed. My heart
thumped like mad as I heard
someone coming up the stairs.

Very slowly the door swung open,
and there stood my mum,
holding a tray of food.

There was an awkward silence,
and then she said

"Here, I've brought your supper,
not that you deserve it."

She picked up my clothes
and began to fold them.

"I've been in that bath for hours,"
she went on, and I breathed

a sigh of relief. "And by the look
of your clothes its your turn now.
I can't think where you go
to get them so dirty."

The next morning I heard
the other side of the story.
My dad had come cycling home
and been picked up by the police—
to go and lower Old Jimmy
and Cloth Cap to the ground.
Then the police found the parcel
and began to ask awkward questions.

My dad's picture was in the paper,
and later on he had to give evidence
at the trial. Both men were sent
to prison for smuggling drugs,
so I had done the right thing
in making sure that my dad didn't
accidentally get mixed up with them.

As for Alf, I let him think
that I had gone straight back home.
I just couldn't risk him talking.

Now you can understand why
I can't tell you the name of this city,
and why I don't mind moths.
That big one certainly did me
a good turn!

The thing that puzzled my dad,
and the police, is how Old Jimmy
and Cloth Cap came to be dangling
at the end of that crane.
Cloth Cap swore that he saw someone
in the cab, but Old Jimmy reckoned
it must have been black magic!

One of these days I'll tell my dad
what really happened that night.

But not just yet.
I get into plenty of hot water
as it is—
Thanks to Old Jimmy's bath!